Mini Pies

Mini Pies

LOVE FOOD™

This edition published in 2011

LOVE FOOD is an imprint of Parragon Books Ltd

Parragon
Queen Street House
4 Queen Street
Bath BA1 1HE, UK

www.parragon.com

ISBN: 978-1-4454-4448-2

Printed in China

Created and produced by Pene Parker and Becca Spry
Author and Home Economist: Sara Lewis
Photographer: Stephen Conroy

Notes for the reader

This book uses both metric and imperial measurements. Follow the same units of measurements
throughout; do not mix metric and imperial. All spoon measurements are level: teaspoons are
assumed to be 5 ml, and tablespoons are assumed to be 15 ml. Unless otherwise stated, milk is
assumed to be full fat, eggs and individual vegetables are medium, and pepper is freshly ground
black pepper.

The times given are an approximate guide only. Preparation times differ according to the techniques
used by different people and the cooking times may also vary from those given. Optional ingredients, variations or serving suggestions have not been included in the calculations.

Recipes using raw or very lightly cooked eggs should be avoided by infants, the elderly, pregnant
women, convalescents, and anyone suffering from an illness. Pregnant and breastfeeding women
are advised to avoid eating peanuts and peanut products. Sufferers from nut allergies should be
aware that some of the ready-made ingredients used in the recipes in this book may contain nuts.
Always check the packaging before use.

Contents

Introduction

These bite-sized pies, made with buttery crumbly pastry, will melt in your mouth. There are tiny pies that are ideal for parties and slightly larger pies that are delicious for a light lunch or dessert. There's something for everyone, from pies made with shortcrust to crunchy biscuit crumb cases and wafer-thin filo delights.

Muffin tins

Tins come with 6, 12 and 24 sections. If using a 6- or 12-section tin you will need to bake 2 or more batches of pies for some of the recipes in this book. Metal tins with a non-stick finish are best, as the metal conducts heat efficiently, producing a crisp crust. Different grades and prices are available. Silicone muffin tins are best kept for muffins and cakes rather than for more fragile pie crusts.

Cookie cutters

You will need a 10-cm/4-inch plain or fluted cookie cutter for the muffin-sized pies and a 6-cm/2½-inch cutter for the mini muffin sized pies, plus slightly smaller cutters for the pie tops. If you don't have the right size, check the tops of your glasses, cups and saucers and cut around these. It is worth buying cookie cutters with different shaped edges and finishes, including tiny novelty shaped cutters such as hearts, flowers, stars, letters and holly leaves.

Cutters for pastry decorations

Make pie lids from flower, heart or circle shapes stamped out with cookie cutters – use these instead of round lids. You can also stamp out tiny versions of these shapes using mini cookie cutters and stick them to your round pastry lid using milk. If you don't have any cutters, cut leaves freehand with a sharp knife.

Pastry wheel

This looks a bit like a scaled-down version of a pizza cutter; buy one with a fluted edge for cutting strips of pastry for lattice-topped pies.

Pastry brushes

Use a clean brush with firmly attached bristles. Ideally have two different-sized ones, one slightly smaller than the other, for glazing and brushing the top edges of the mini muffin sized pies. Wash your brushes after use in warm soapy water and dry well before storing.

Oven thermometers

Ovens vary greatly in their accuracy, with some fan ovens being very hot. Monitor your oven with a small oven thermometer; they are inexpensive and widely available from cookshops and hardware stores. Simply hang the thermometer from a shelf so it reads the temperature in the centre of your oven.

The importance of chilling pastry

Chilling the pastry after making it enables the dough to relax and so minimizes the chances of it shrinking during cooking. Shrinkage is most obvious when making a single crust pie that is baked blind. Well chilled pastry is also much easier to roll out.

Baking blind

'Baking blind' means to bake a pie or tart without a filling, and it is done to stop the filling from soaking through the pastry during cooking and producing a soggy-bottomed pie. Soggy pastry not only affects the taste of the pie, but also makes it hard to remove it from the tin. Roll out and line sections of a muffin tin with pastry, then prick the base with a fork once or twice and chill again for 15 minutes. Line the pastry with baking paper a little larger than the tin (crumple the paper up before using to make it easier to fit). Half-fill with baking beans (available from cookshops), small dried pasta shapes or dried pulses, to keep the pastry in shape for muffin sized pie cases. Bake at 190°C/375°F/Gas Mark 5 for 10 minutes, then remove the paper and beans and cook for 2–3 minutes more, until the cases are crisp and dry. Allow the beans, pasta or pulses to cool, then store them. Add the filling to the pies and continue to cook as per the recipe. Mini muffin sized pies are so tiny that they don't need baking blind.

How to tell if a pie is cooked

Cooking times are given as a guide, but it is wise to check on the progress of your pies during baking. If your oven seems too hot and your pies are browning too quickly, protect the tops with a piece of foil or reduce the temperature slightly. Your pies may look ready on the top, but it is important that the bottom crust is also cooked through.

Ready-made shortcrust pastry

While it's great to make your own shortcrust pastry, sometimes there just isn't the time. Keep a supply of ready-made shortcrust or pie dough in the freezer, or buy it from the chiller cabinet in the supermarket.

Filo pastry

Ready-made wafer-thin filo pastry is so good that it isn't worth making your own. Packs vary in size, but if buying frozen you will need to defrost the whole pack. Separate the sheets, use as many as you need, then wrap the rest in clingfilm, put them back in the box and refreeze. (This product is the only exception to the rule about not refreezing – it is perfectly safe to do so, providing it is out of the freezer for the minimum time.) If the sheet sizes are different to those specified in the recipes, keep to the size of the trimmed squares/rectangles specified. Filo pastry is so thin that it dries out very quickly, so don't unwrap it until the very last minute and ideally unfold sheets so that they are flat, then cover them with clingfilm and just remove 1 sheet at a time as you cut and shape it.

Lattice pastry decorations

Cut ultra-thin or finger-width strips of pastry with a small knife or fluted-edged pastry wheel and either arrange over the pies in 2 layers or interweave different strips for a basketweave effect. Symmetrically arranged strips add form, while randomly arranged strips at converging angles add a more modern twist.

Crimped edges

Decorate the edges of double-crust pies by placing your finger and thumb close together, then drawing the edge of the pastry inwards with the blade of a small knife to give a scalloped edge.

Forked edges

A quick, homely finish can be made by pressing the tines of a fork against the edges of a double-crust pie.

Different toppings

Pies don't have to be topped with pastry; sprinkle with crumble, flapjack or granola or whirls of soft meringue. Add whipped cream to cooled pies and drizzle with toffee, melted chocolate, honey or maple syrup.

Egg yolk and water glaze

Beat 1 egg yolk with 1 tablespoon of cold water, then brush this over the tops of the pies using a pastry brush. This produces a burnished gold-topped glaze. Sprinkle with a little sugar before baking if you wish. Traditional cooks used to say that an egg yolk glaze should only be used for savoury pies, but you can use it for sweet if you wish.

Egg white and caster sugar glaze

This produces a more traditional, paler-coloured finish for sweet pies. Brush the tops with a little egg white, then sprinkle with caster sugar before baking.

Milk and caster sugar glaze

This produces a paler coloured finish for sweet pies, not dissimilar to the egg white and sugar glaze above. Brush the tops with a little milk, then sprinkle with caster sugar before baking. For a caramelized sugar glaze if you are making an open-topped pie, dot the fruit with a little butter and sprinkle with sugar; dust heavily with sifted icing sugar towards the end of cooking and return to the oven for the last 5 minutes, until the sugar has dissolved and caramelized to a deep golden colour.

Shortcrust pastry or pie dough

Makes: 625 g/1 lb 6 oz, or
enough for 12 muffin
sized pies, or 1 quantity
Prep: 25 minutes

350 g/12 oz plain flour, plus
extra for dusting

55 g/2 oz caster sugar, optional

85 g/3 oz unsalted butter,
chilled and diced

85 g/3 oz vegetable
shortening, chilled and diced

4–4½ tbsp cold water

The most versatile, everyday pastry, this is great for sweet pies — or simply omit the sugar for savoury tarts. Mix by hand or blitz in a food processor. The key is to use just enough water to bind the pastry for a wonderful crumbly texture that melts in the mouth.

1. To make by hand: put the flour and sugar (if making sweet shortcrust) in a mixing bowl, then add the butter and shortening. Toss together, then lift the mixture and rub it through your fingers and thumbs. Continue scooping up the mixture and rubbing until it looks like breadcrumbs. Gradually mix in the water with a round-bladed knife, then squeeze the mixture together with your hands until it forms a smooth dough.

To make with an electric mixer or food processor: put the flour, sugar, butter and shortening in a bowl and mix together using the electric mixer, or add to a processor bowl fitted with a plastic or metal blade and mix briefly. It should resemble breadcrumbs. Gradually add the water with the machine running and mix briefly until it just comes together in a ball.

2. Wrap the pastry in clingfilm or put it into a small plastic bag, and chill in the fridge for 15 minutes. Knead the pastry lightly on a surface dusted with flour, then roll it out thinly. Using a plain or fluted cookie cutter, stamp out circles 10 cm/4 inches in diameter and use to line a 12-section deep muffin tin. Alternatively stamp out circles 6 cm/2½ inches in diameter and use to line 2 x 12-section mini muffin tins. When you can cut no more circles, squeeze the trimmings into a ball, then reroll this out and cut round lids, strips for lattice tops or tiny shapes.

Tips

Keep everything as cold as possible. Use butter and vegetable shortening straight from the fridge. If your hands feel hot, rinse them in cold water before you begin. Use cold water to bind. A marble pastry board is useful (but not essential) for keeping the pastry cold while rolling out.

Don't add too much liquid. Use just enough to bind the crumbs. For shortcrust/pie dough you need 1 teaspoon of water for every 25 g/1 oz of mixture. For larger quantities change to tablespoons (1 tablespoon = 3 teaspoons). If you use too much water, the pastry will be hard.

Avoid over-flouring the work surface. Aim for the lightest of dustings and rub a little flour over the rolling pin. Before turning the pastry, loosen it with a long flexible palette knife.

All butter pastry

Based on French 'pâte sucrée', this pastry has a higher ratio of sugar than shortcrust, is made with all butter and bound with egg yolks for richness.

Makes: 650 g/1 lb 7 oz, or enough for 12 muffin sized pies, or 1 quantity

Prep: 25 minutes

350 g/12 oz plain flour, plus extra for dusting

85 g/3 oz icing sugar

175 g/6 oz unsalted butter, at room temperature, diced

4 egg yolks

1. To make by hand: spoon the flour on to the work surface, then sprinkle the sugar over the top. Mix together, then make a well in the centre and add the butter and yolks. Work the butter and yolks together with the fingers of one hand. Gradually draw in a little flour, working your fingertips in a circular motion but being careful not to let the yolk escape through the flour; use your other hand to flick a little flour around the edges so the yolks stay contained. Blend until almost of the flour has been incorporated, then knead in the last bits until you have a smooth ball.

To make with an electric mixer or food processor: put the sugar and butter in a bowl and mix together using the electric mixer, or add to a processor bowl fitted with a plastic or metal blade and mix briefly. Add the egg yolks and a little of the flour and beat until smooth, then add the remaining flour and mix to make a smooth dough.

2. Wrap in clingfilm or put into a small plastic bag, chill in the fridge for 15 minutes, then roll out and shape as in point 2 of the method on page 8.

Tips
This pastry requires careful handling. Always chill it when it is first made, and again when it is shaped. If it is too soft to roll out, roll it out thinly between 2 sheets of baking paper.

Variations for Shortcrust and All butter pastry

Cinnamon:	Add 1 teaspoon of ground cinnamon with the sugar.
Chocolate:	Make with 325 g/11½ oz plain flour and 25 g/1 oz sifted cocoa powder.
Hazelnut:	Toast 55 g/2 oz hazelnuts until golden. Chop them finely and add with the sugar.
Herb:	Omit the sugar, add 2 tablespoons of chopped fresh rosemary, parsley or chives and salt and pepper.
Lemon/Orange:	Add grated rind of 1 lemon or orange with the sugar.
Mustard:	Omit the sugar, add 2 teaspoons of dry English mustard powder and a little salt and pepper.

1

2.

Party Pies

Summer fruit pies

Makes: 24 mini muffin sized pies
Prep: 30 minutes
Cook: 15 minutes

a little butter, for greasing

350 g/12 oz mixed strawberries, raspberries and redcurrants

2 tsp cornflour

3 tbsp caster sugar, plus extra for sprinkling

grated rind of ½ lemon

450 g/1 lb Sweet Shortcrust Pastry (see page 8) or ready-made sweet shortcrust pastry, chilled

a little plain flour, for dusting

1 egg yolk mixed with 1 tbsp water, to glaze

whipped cream, to serve

Celebrate the summer with these gorgeous red fruit pies. The soft fruit contrasts deliciously with the crisp pastry.

1. Preheat the oven to 180°C/350°F/Gas Mark 4. Lightly grease 2 x 12-section mini muffin tins.

2. Roughly chop the strawberries and break up large raspberries. Put all the fruit in a mixing bowl and stir in the cornflour, sugar and lemon rind.

3. Roll the pastry out thinly on a lightly floured surface. Using a fluted cookie cutter, stamp out 24 circles, each 6 cm/2½ inches in diameter. Press these gently into the prepared tins, rerolling the trimmings as needed. Reserve some of the trimmings for decoration.

4. Brush the top edges of the pie cases with a little of the egg glaze, then spoon in the filling.

5. Roll the reserved pastry out thinly on a lightly floured surface. Cut strips 1 cm/½ inch wide. Arrange 2 strips over each pie, pressing the edges together well to seal, then use a cookie cutter to cut small stars and arrange these over the strips. Brush egg glaze over the pastry and sprinkle with a little sugar.

6. Bake in the preheated oven for 15 minutes, or until golden. Leave to cool in the tins for 10 minutes, then loosen with a round-bladed knife and transfer to a wire rack to cool. Serve warm or cold with whipped cream.

Valentine berry love pies

Makes: 24 mini muffin sized pies
Prep: 30 minutes
Cook: 15 minutes

a little butter, for greasing

350 g/12 oz strawberries

2 tsp cornflour

2 tbsp strawberry jam

grated rind of 2 limes

450 g/1 lb All Butter Pastry
(see page 9) or ready-made
sweet shortcrust pastry,
chilled

a little plain flour, for dusting

1 egg yolk mixed with 1 tbsp
water, to glaze

a little caster sugar, for
sprinkling

TO SERVE

225 ml/8 fl oz double cream

grated rind of 2 limes

2 tbsp icing sugar

These dainty pies are delicious while warm. If you can find a passion fruit in the shops, cut it in half and scoop out the seeds over the whipped cream topping just before serving.

1. Preheat the oven to 180°C/350°F/Gas Mark 4. Lightly grease 2 x 12-section mini muffin tins.

2. Roughly chop the strawberries. Put them in a mixing bowl and stir in the cornflour, jam and lime rind.

3. Roll half the pastry out thinly on a lightly floured surface. Using a fluted cookie cutter, stamp out 24 circles, each 6 cm/2½ inches in diameter. Press these gently into the prepared tins, rerolling the trimmings as needed.

4. Brush the top edges of the pie cases with a little of the egg glaze, then spoon in the filling.

5. Roll the reserved pastry out thinly on a lightly floured surface. Stamp out 24 circles, each 5 cm/2 inches in diameter, rerolling the trimmings as needed. Use a cookie cutter to cut hearts from each circle, some tiny, some bigger. Use the rounds and bigger hearts as lids, pressing the edges together. Brush egg glaze over the pastry and sprinkle with caster sugar.

6. Bake in the preheated oven for 15 minutes, or until golden. Leave to cool in the tins for 10 minutes, then loosen with a round-bladed knife and transfer to a wire rack to cool. Whip the cream until it forms soft swirls, then fold in half the lime rind and all the icing sugar. Sprinkle with the rest of the lime rind. Serve spoonfuls of the cream with the pies.

Deep South cherry pies

Makes: 24 mini muffin sized pies
Prep: 30 minutes
Cook: 15 minutes

a little butter, for greasing

350 g/12 oz cherries, stoned
and halved, plus extra to
decorate

2 tsp cornflour

3 tbsp caster sugar

1 tsp vanilla extract

½ tsp ground cinnamon

450 g/1 lb Sweet Shortcrust
Pastry (see page 8) or
ready-made sweet shortcrust
pastry, chilled

a little plain flour, for dusting

1 egg yolk mixed with 1 tbsp
water, to glaze

2 tbsp caster sugar mixed
with a large pinch ground
cinnamon, for sprinkling

These are sure to evoke happy memories of childhood. They're delicious served still hot from the oven with a drizzle of custard or spoonful of vanilla ice cream.

1. Preheat the oven to 180°C/350°F/Gas Mark 4. Lightly grease 2 x 12-section mini muffin tins.

2. Put the stoned cherries in a mixing bowl and stir in the cornflour, sugar, vanilla extract and cinnamon.

3. Roll two-thirds of the pastry out thinly on a lightly floured surface. Using a fluted cookie cutter, stamp out 24 circles, each 6 cm/2½ inches in diameter. Press these into the prepared tins, rerolling the trimmings as needed.

4. Brush the top edges of the pie cases with a little of the egg glaze, then spoon in the filling.

5. Roll the reserved pastry out thinly on a lightly floured surface. Stamp out 24 circles, each 5 cm/2 inches in diameter, rerolling the trimmings as needed. Arrange these on top of the pies, pressing the edges together to seal. Brush over some egg glaze. Use a cookie cutter to cut tiny hearts and flowers from the remaining pastry and arrange these on the lids. Brush egg glaze over the decorations.

6. Bake in the preheated oven for 15 minutes, or until golden. Leave to cool in the tins for 10 minutes, then loosen with a round-bladed knife and transfer to a wire rack to cool. Serve warm or cold, sprinkled with the cinnamon mixture, on a plate decorated with extra cherries.

Peach and chocolate meringue pies

Makes: 6 muffin sized pies
Prep: 40 minutes
Cook: 22-25 minutes

225 g/8 oz All Butter Hazelnut
Pastry (see page 9) or
ready-made sweet shortcrust
pastry, chilled

a little plain flour, for dusting

25 g/1 oz butter, plus extra
for greasing

2 peaches, peeled if liked, halved,
stoned and diced

50 g/1¾ oz dark chocolate,
roughly chopped

2 egg whites

55 g/2 oz caster sugar

What is there not to like? Crisp hazelnut pastry with a slightly tart peach filling that contrasts with a soft cloud of sweet meringue swirled with melted dark chocolate. You don't need to add anything, not even cream.

1. Lightly grease a 6-section muffin tin. Roll the pastry out thinly on a lightly floured surface. Using a plain cookie cutter, stamp out 6 circles each 10 cm/4 inches in diameter. Press these gently into the prepared tin, rerolling the trimmings as needed. Prick the base of each pie with a fork, then chill in the fridge for 15 minutes. Preheat the oven to 190°C/375°F/Gas Mark 5.

2. Line the pastry cases with squares of crumpled baking paper and baking beans (see page 6). Bake in the preheated oven for 10 minutes. Remove the paper and beans and cook the pastry cases for 2–3 minutes more, or until the base of the pastry is crisp and dry.

3. Meanwhile, melt the butter in a small frying pan or saucepan, add the peaches and cook gently for 5 minutes, stirring occasionally, until softened. Spoon the peaches into the pastry cases.

4. Put the chocolate in a heatproof bowl, set over a saucepan of gently simmering water and heat until melted. Whisk the egg whites in a large clean mixing bowl until you have stiff, moist-looking peaks, then gradually whisk in the sugar a teaspoon at a time for another 1-2 minutes, or until the meringue is very thick and glossy. Fold the melted chocolate into the meringue with just a couple of swirls of the spoon for a marbled effect. Spoon into the pies.

5. Bake in the preheated oven for 5-7 minutes, or until the meringue peaks are golden and just cooked through. Leave to cool in the tin for 10 minutes, then loosen with a round-bladed knife and transfer to a wire rack to cool. Serve warm.

Brandy apple pies

Makes: 24 mini muffin sized pies
Prep: 35 minutes
Cook: 23–25 minutes

These dainty little high-topped pies have been personalized by adding an initial made from a tiny rope of pastry for each of your dinner guests; if you have a set of little alphabet cutters then you may prefer to use these. If you wish, cook these pies in advance and freeze when cool, then warm through when needed.

450 g/1 lb cooking apples, quartered, cored, peeled and diced

25 g/1 oz butter, plus extra for greasing

55 g/2 oz caster sugar, plus extra for sprinkling

55 g/2 oz sultanas or raisins

grated rind of 1 lemon

3 tbsp Bourbon or brandy

1 quantity All Butter Pastry (see page 9) or ready-made sweet shortcrust pastry, chilled

a little plain flour, for dusting

a little milk, to glaze

whipped cream, to serve

1. Preheat the oven to 180°C/350°F/Gas Mark 4. Lightly grease 2 x 12-section mini muffin tins.

2. Put the apples in a medium saucepan with the butter, sugar, sultanas and lemon rind. Cook, uncovered, over a gentle heat, stirring from time to time, for 8–10 minutes, or until the apples have softened but still hold their shape. Add the Bourbon and cook until just bubbling. Keeping it over the heat, flame with a taper or long match, stand well back and cook for a minute or so, until the flame subsides. Leave the mixture to cool.

3. Roll half the pastry out thinly on a lightly floured surface. Using a fluted cookie cutter, stamp out 24 circles, each 6 cm/2½ inches in diameter. Press these gently into the prepared tins, rerolling the trimmings as needed.

4. Brush the top edges of the pie cases with milk, then spoon in the filling, doming it up high in the centre.

5. Roll the reserved pastry out thinly on a lightly floured surface. Stamp out 24 circles, the same size as before, rerolling the trimmings as needed. Arrange these on top of the pies, pressing the edges together well to seal. Brush milk over the pastry.

6. Shape tiny ropes from the remaining pastry into the initials of your dinner guests or family. Press these onto the pie tops, brush with a little extra milk and sprinkle with sugar.

7. Bake in the preheated oven for 15 minutes, or until golden. Leave to cool in the tins for 10 minutes, then loosen with a round-bladed knife and transfer to a wire rack to cool. Serve warm or cold, sprinkled with a little extra sugar, with spoonfuls of whipped cream.

Hot spiced pumpkin pies

Makes: 24 mini muffin sized pies
Prep: 30 minutes
Cook: 30 minutes

a little butter, for greasing

250 g/9 oz pumpkin (weighed after deseeding and peeling), diced small

4 tbsp semi-skimmed milk

2 eggs

3 tbsp runny honey

1 tsp ground ginger

¼ tsp ground mixed spice

325 g/11½ oz All Butter Pastry (see page 9) or ready-made sweet shortcrust pastry, chilled

a little plain flour, for dusting

a little milk, to glaze

a little caster sugar, for sprinkling

These are always popular for Halloween. Serve them as they are or top with a spoonful of whipped cream flavoured with a little honey or maple syrup.

1. Preheat the oven to 190°C/375°F/Gas Mark 5. Lightly grease 2 x 12-section mini muffin tins.

2. Put the pumpkin in a steamer, cover and set over a pan of gently simmering water. Steam for 15 minutes, or until tender. Purée with the milk in a liquidizer or food processor until smooth. Cool slightly, then mix in the eggs, honey, ginger and mixed spice.

3. Roll the pastry out thinly on a lightly floured surface. Using a plain cookie cutter, stamp out 24 circles, each 6 cm/2½ inches in diameter. Press these gently into the tins, rerolling the trimmings as needed. Squeeze any remaining trimmings together and reserve.

4. Brush the top edges of the pie cases with milk, then spoon in the filling.

5. Roll the remaining pastry trimmings out thinly on a lightly floured surface. Use a sharp knife to cut tiny leaves and mark on veins. Brush these with milk, arrange them over each pie and sprinkle with a little sugar.

6. Bake in the preheated oven for 15 minutes, or until the leaves are golden and the filling is just set. Leave to cool in the tins for 10 minutes, then loosen with a round-bladed knife and transfer to a wire rack to cool. Serve warm or cold, sprinkled with a little extra sugar.

Christmas cranberry and orange pies

Makes: 12 mini muffin sized pies
Prep: 30 minutes
Cook: 30 minutes

Cranberries needn't be kept just for sauce to go with the turkey; try them gently poached with star anise for a fragrant filling in an orange-scented pie crust. The secret to cooking cranberries is not to add sugar at first, but instead when the skins have softened. For a festive accompaniment serve with whipped cream flavoured with orange liqueur.

a little butter, for greasing

175 g/6 oz frozen cranberries

1 tbsp cornflour

3 tbsp freshly squeezed orange juice

2 star anise

55 g/2 oz caster sugar, plus extra for sprinkling

225 g/8 oz Orange Sweet Shortcrust Pastry (see pages 8–9) or ready-made sweet shortcrust pastry, chilled

a little plain flour, for dusting

a little milk, to glaze

a little caster sugar, for sprinkling

1. Preheat the oven to 180°C/350°F/Gas Mark 4. Lightly grease a 12-section mini muffin tin.

2. Put the still-frozen cranberries in a medium saucepan with the cornflour and orange juice. Add the star anise and cook uncovered over a low heat, stirring from time to time, for 5 minutes, or until the cranberries have softened. Add the sugar and cook for 5 minutes more, then leave to cool.

3. Roll the pastry out thinly on a lightly floured surface. Using a fluted cookie cutter, stamp out 12 circles, each 6 cm/2½ inches in diameter. Press these gently into the prepared tin, rerolling the trimmings as needed. Squeeze any remaining trimmings together and reserve.

4. Brush the top edges of the pie cases with a little milk. Discard the star anise, then spoon in the filling.

5. Roll the remaining pastry out thinly on a lightly floured surface. Using a fluted pastry wheel, cut thin strips of pastry. Arrange these over each pie and brush with a little milk. Sprinkle with a little sugar. Bake in the preheated oven for 20 minutes, covering with foil after 10 minutes if the tops are browning too quickly. Leave to cool in the tin for 10 minutes, then loosen with a round-bladed knife and transfer to a wire rack to cool. Serve warm or cold.

Shaker lemon pies

Makes: 24 mini muffin sized pies
Prep: 40 minutes
Cook: 55 minutes

These are traditionally made with thin-skinned Meyer lemons soaked for hours in sugar before baking, but as they are notoriously difficult to find, ordinary lemons have been used here instead. To get around the increased bitterness, two lemons are thinly sliced and poached in a sugar syrup, then mixed with extra grated lemon rind and juice for a tangy filling.

3½ medium lemons

250 g/9 oz caster sugar, plus extra for sprinkling

4 tbsp water

60 g/2¼ oz butter, plus extra for greasing

3 eggs

450 g/1 lb All Butter Pastry (see page 9) or ready-made sweet shortcrust pastry, chilled

a little plain flour, for dusting

egg white, to glaze

1. Lightly grease 2 x 12-section mini muffin tins. Thinly slice 2 of the lemons – you need 24 slices. Put them in a medium saucepan with 100 g/3½ oz the sugar and the water and stir. Cook uncovered over a low heat, stirring from time to time, for 30 minutes, or until the lemon slices are soft and translucent and only just beginning to lose their colour. Using a fork, scoop the lemon slices out of the saucepan, draining off the syrup, and put them on a plate; they will be used in step 5.

2. Preheat the oven to 180°C/350°F/Gas Mark 4. Grate the rind and squeeze the juice from the remaining lemons. Add them to the syrup with the butter and remaining sugar. Heat gently, uncovered, until the butter is just melted.

3. Meanwhile, beat the eggs in a small bowl. Remove the pan from the heat and strain the eggs through a sieve into it, stirring well. Return to the heat and cook very gently for 10 minutes, stirring frequently, or until the mixture has thickened and is jam-like. Increase the heat if needed but keep a watchful eye; too hot and the eggs will curdle. Leave to cool.

4. Roll half the pastry out thinly on a lightly floured surface. Using a fluted cookie cutter, stamp out 24 circles, each 6 cm/2½ inches in diameter. Press these gently into the prepared tins, rerolling trimmings as needed.

5. Brush the top edges of the cases with a little egg white, then spoon in the filling. Top each with a slice of the candied lemon made in step 1.

6. Roll the reserved pastry out thinly on a lightly floured surface. Stamp out 24 circles, each 5 cm/2 inches in diameter, rerolling the trimmings as needed. Press these on to the pie tops, pressing the edges together well.

7. Make 4 small cuts in the top of each pie, brush the pies with egg white and sprinkle with sugar. Bake in the preheated oven for 15 minutes, or until golden. Leave to cool in the tins for 10 minutes, then loosen with a round-bladed knife and transfer to a wire rack to cool. Serve warm or cold.

Lemon meringue pies

Makes: 12 muffin sized pies
Prep: 30 minutes
Cook: 18–22 minutes

100 g/3½ oz butter, plus extra for greasing

2 tbsp golden syrup

300 g/10½ oz graham crackers or digestive biscuits, crushed

grated rind and juice of 3 lemons

200 g/7 oz caster sugar

40 g/1½ oz cornflour

3 eggs, separated

This all-time classic is loved by everyone, with its sharp tangy lemon filling topped generously with piped or spooned meringue. These are made with a crumb crust.

1. Preheat the oven to 180°C/350°F/Gas Mark 4. Lightly grease a 12-section muffin tin.

2. Put the butter and syrup in a small saucepan and heat until the butter has just melted. Take the pan off the heat, stir in the biscuit crumbs, then divide the mixture between the sections of the prepared tin. Press it firmly over the base and sides of the tin with the back of a teaspoon.

3. Line the cases with baking paper and baking beans, then bake them in the preheated oven for 8–10 minutes, or until slightly darker in colour. Leave to cool and harden in the tin for 10–15 minutes. Remove the paper and beans.

4. Put the lemon rind in a second, slightly larger saucepan. Make the juice up to 450 ml/16 fl oz with cold water, then add this liquid to the rind and bring just to the boil. In a mixing bowl, stir 85 g/3 oz sugar, the cornflour and egg yolks together until a thick paste has formed, then gradually stir in the boiling lemon juice until smooth.

5. Pour the liquid back into the saucepan and cook over a medium heat, stirring constantly, for a few minutes, until it is very thick and smooth. Spoon the filling into the crumb cases.

6. For the topping, whisk the egg whites in a large clean mixing bowl until you have stiff peaks, then gradually whisk in the remaining sugar a teaspoon at a time for another 1–2 minutes, or until the meringue is very thick and glossy. Spoon or pipe the meringue on top of the pies.

7. Bake in the preheated oven for 10–12 minutes, or until the meringue peaks are golden and just cooked through. Leave to cool and firm up in the tin, then loosen with a round-bladed knife and transfer to a plate.

S'more pies

Makes: 12 mini muffin sized pies
Prep: 20 minutes
Cook: 9-10 minutes

This summer camp favourite gets the grown-up treatment. Mini crumb cases flavoured with peanut butter, then filled with a rich dark chocolate cream and piled high with mini marshmallows. Great with cups of strong coffee or hot chocolate at the end of a barbecue.

40 g/1½ oz butter, plus extra for greasing

1 tbsp crunchy peanut butter

85 g/3 oz graham crackers or Rich Tea biscuits, crushed

100 g/3½ oz plain chocolate, roughly chopped

1 tbsp icing sugar

6 tbsp double cream

40 g/1½ oz mini marshmallows

1. Preheat the oven to 180°C/350°F/Gas Mark 4. Lightly grease a 12-section mini muffin tin.

2. Put the butter in a small saucepan. Gently heat, uncovered, until it has melted. Take the saucepan off the heat and stir in the peanut butter, then the biscuit crumbs. Divide between the sections of the prepared tin. Press it firmly over the base and sides of the tin with the back of a teaspoon.

3. Bake in the preheated oven for 6 minutes, or until slightly darker in colour. Reshape the centre if needed with the back of a spoon. Leave to cool and harden in the tin for 10-15 minutes.

4. Meanwhile, put the chocolate in a heatproof bowl, set the bowl over a saucepan of gently simmering water and heat until melted. Add the sugar and gradually stir in the cream until smooth. Preheat the grill to medium.

5. Spoon the filling into the cases. Sprinkle the mini marshmallows over the top and press them lightly into the chocolate so they don't roll off.

6. Grill for 3-4 minutes, or until the marshmallows have softened and are just beginning to colour. Leave to cool in the tin for 30 minutes, then loosen with a round-bladed knife and carefully lift out of the tin. Serve.

Tiny Tartlets

Blueberry tarts

Makes: 24 mini muffin sized pies
Prep: 25 minutes
Cook: 17–18 minutes

300 g/10½ oz blueberries

2 tsp cornflour

55 g/2 oz caster sugar

4 tsp water

55 g/2 oz plain flour, plus extra
for dusting

grated rind of 1 lemon

40 g/1½ oz butter, diced, plus
extra for greasing

325 g/11½ oz All Butter Pastry
(see page 9) or ready-made sweet
shortcrust pastry, chilled

*Crisp, dainty pies with a moist blueberry filling
and a buttery crumble top. Serve while still warm,
with good vanilla ice cream.*

1. Preheat the oven to 190°C/375°F/Gas Mark 5. Lightly grease
2 x 12-section mini muffin tins.

2. Put half the blueberries in a small saucepan with the cornflour, half the
caster sugar and the water. Cook, uncovered, over a medium heat, stirring
constantly, for 2–3 minutes, or until the juices begin to run and the sauce
thickens. Take the pan off the heat and add the remaining blueberries.

3. For the streusel, put the flour, lemon rind, butter and remaining sugar
in a medium mixing bowl. Toss together, then lift the mixture and rub it
through your fingers and thumbs until it looks like fine breadcrumbs.

4. Roll the pastry out thinly on a lightly floured surface. Using a fluted
cookie cutter, stamp out 24 circles each 6 cm/2½ inches in diameter.
Press these into the prepared tins, rerolling trimmings as needed. Spoon
the blueberry filling into the cases, then sprinkle the tops of the tarts with
the streusel mixture.

5. Bake in the preheated oven for 15 minutes, or until the topping is pale
gold. Leave to cool in the tins for 10 minutes, then loosen with a
round-bladed knife and transfer to a wire rack to cool. Serve warm or cold.

Orchard tarts

Makes: 6 muffin sized pies
Prep: 45 minutes
Cook: 32–33 minutes

Apple pies with a twist; they are sprinkled with homemade granola (a mix of oats, seeds and nuts). Mix and match the topping ingredients to suit your larder; try barley flakes, flaked almonds, chopped macadamia nuts, golden linseeds or pumpkin seeds.

a little butter, for greasing

225 g/8 oz All Butter Pastry (see page 9) or ready-made sweet shortcrust pastry, chilled

a little plain flour, for dusting

1 pear, about 150 g/5½ oz, quartered, cored, peeled and diced

1 cooking apple, about 150 g/5½ oz, quartered, cored, peeled and diced

3 ripe red plums, halved, stoned and diced

25 g/1 oz caster sugar

1 tbsp water

1 tbsp sunflower oil

1 tbsp runny honey

4 tbsp porridge oats

1 tbsp sesame seeds

2 tbsp sunflower seeds

2 tbsp pumpkin seeds

2 tbsp hazelnuts, roughly chopped

1. Lightly grease a 6-section muffin tin. Roll the pastry out thinly on a lightly floured surface. Using a plain cookie cutter, stamp out 6 circles each 10 cm/4 inches in diameter. Press these gently into the prepared tin, rerolling the trimmings as needed. Prick the base of each with a fork, then chill in the fridge for 15 minutes. Preheat the oven to 190°C/375°F/Gas Mark 5.

2. Line the pastry cases with squares of crumpled baking paper and baking beans (see page 6). Bake in the preheated oven for 10 minutes. Remove the paper and beans and cook the cases for 2–3 minutes more, or until the base of the pastry is crisp and dry. Turn the oven down to 180°C/350°F/Gas Mark 4.

3. Put all the fruit, sugar and water in a medium saucepan. Cover and cook over a gentle heat, stirring, for 5 minutes, or until the fruit has just softened. Meanwhile, for the granola, warm the oil and honey in a frying pan. Stir in the oats, seeds and hazelnuts and set aside. Spoon the fruit into the cases, then sprinkle the granola on top.

4. Bake in the preheated oven for 20 minutes, covering with foil after 10 minutes if the granola is browning too quickly. Leave to cool in the tin for 10 minutes, then loosen with a round-bladed knife and transfer to a wire rack to cool. Serve warm.

Caramelized apple tarts

Makes: 12 muffin sized pies
Prep: 45 minutes
Cook: 32–36 minutes

These French-inspired tarts are filled with a tangy apple and lemon custard, then topped with wafer-thin sliced apples and glazed with a little icing sugar. They can be tricky to remove from the tin as the sugar glaze makes them sticky, so do take extra care.

450 g/1 lb Sweet Shortcrust Pastry (see page 8) or ready-made sweet shortcrust pastry, chilled

a little plain flour, for dusting

5 Granny Smith apples, quartered, cored and peeled

85 g/3 oz caster sugar

finely grated rind and juice of 1 lemon

2 eggs

15 g/½ oz butter, plus extra for greasing

3 tbsp icing sugar, sifted

1. Lightly grease a 12-section muffin tin. Roll the pastry out thinly on a lightly floured surface. Using a plain cookie cutter, stamp out 12 circles, each 10 cm/4 inches in diameter. Press these gently into the prepared tin, rerolling the trimmings as needed. Prick the base of each with a fork, then chill in the fridge for 15 minutes. Preheat the oven to 190°C/375°F/Gas Mark 5.

2. Line the pastry cases with squares of crumpled baking paper and baking beans (see page 6). Bake in the preheated oven for 10 minutes. Remove the paper and beans and cook the cases for 2–3 minutes more, or until the base of the pastry is crisp and dry. Turn the oven down to 180°C/350°F/Gas Mark 4.

3. Roughly grate 8 of the apple quarters into a mixing bowl. Add two-thirds of the caster sugar, all the lemon rind and juice and the eggs and whisk together. Spoon the filling into the cases.

4. Thinly slice the remaining apples and arrange them overlapping on top of the pies. Sprinkle with the remaining caster sugar and then dot the pies with the butter.

5. Bake in the preheated oven for 20–25 minutes, or until the filling is set and the sliced apples are browned around the edges.

6. Dust with the icing sugar and return the pies to the oven for 5 minutes, or until the sugar has caramelized. Leave to cool in the tin for 15 minutes, then loosen with a round-bladed knife and transfer to a wire rack to cool. Serve warm or cold.

Mississippi mud pies

Makes: 6 muffin sized pies
Prep: 30 minutes
Cook: 12–13 minutes

a little butter, for greasing

225 g/8 oz Chocolate or Hazelnut
Sweet Shortcrust Pastry
(see pages 8–9) or ready-made
sweet shortcrust pastry, chilled

a little plain flour, for dusting

100 g/3½ oz plain chocolate,
roughly chopped

4 tbsp icing sugar

125 ml/4 fl oz semi-skimmed milk

1 egg

225 ml/8 fl oz double cream

1 tsp vanilla extract

white and dark chocolate curls,
to decorate

A dark, rich, almost truffle-like chocolate layer encased in an even darker crisp chocolate pastry, then topped with soft swirls of Chantilly cream.

1. Lightly grease a 6-section muffin tin. Roll the pastry out thinly on a lightly floured surface. Using a plain cookie cutter, stamp out 6 circles each 10 cm/4 inches in diameter. Press these gently into the prepared tin, rerolling the trimmings as needed. Prick the base of each with a fork, then chill in the fridge for 15 minutes. Preheat the oven to 190°C/375°F/Gas Mark 5.

2. Line the pastry cases with squares of crumpled baking paper and baking beans (see page 6). Bake in the preheated oven for 10 minutes. Remove the paper and beans and cook the cases for 2–3 minutes more, or until the base of the pastry is crisp and dry.

3. Meanwhile, put the plain chocolate in a heatproof bowl, set the bowl over a saucepan of gently simmering water and heat until melted. Beat 2 tablespoons of sugar, the milk and egg together in a jug. Take the bowl of chocolate off the heat and gradually stir in the milk mixture until smooth. Pour the filling into the cases and leave to cool. Transfer the pies to the fridge for 2 hours, or until the filling has set.

4. Whip the cream with the remaining icing sugar and the vanilla until it forms soft folds. Loosen the pastry cases with a round-bladed knife and lift them onto a plate. Spoon the cream over the top and decorate with the chocolate curls.

Chocolate and pecan tarts

Makes: 24 mini muffin sized pies
Prep: 25 minutes
Cook: 20 minutes

These pies freeze well packed into a plastic box. Once defrosted, add a dusting of icing sugar and a drizzle of melted chocolate before serving. Alternatively, warm them in the oven and serve with whipped cream flavoured with ground cinnamon or Greek yogurt and honey.

115 g/4 oz golden syrup

70 g/2½ oz light muscovado sugar

25 g/1 oz butter, plus extra for greasing

50 g/1¾ oz dark chocolate, roughly chopped

325 g/11½ oz All Butter Cinnamon Pastry (see page 9) or ready-made sweet shortcrust pastry, chilled

a little plain flour, for dusting

1 egg, beaten

1 egg yolk

85 g/3 oz pecan nuts

50 g/1¾ oz dark chocolate, roughly chopped, to decorate

1. Preheat the oven to 180°C/350°F/Gas Mark 4. Lightly grease a 2 x 12-section mini muffin tins.

2. Put the syrup, sugar and butter in a small saucepan. Heat gently, uncovered, stirring from time to time, until the butter has just melted. Add the chocolate and stir until it too has melted. Leave to cool slightly.

3. Roll the pastry out thinly on a lightly floured surface. Using a fluted cookie cutter, stamp out 24 circles each 6 cm/2½ inches in diameter. Press these gently into the prepared tins, rerolling the trimmings as needed.

4. Stir the egg and egg yolk into the cooled chocolate mixture until smooth, then spoon this filling into the cases. Decorate the top of each pie with 2 pecan nuts.

5. Bake in the preheated oven for 20 minutes, or until the filling has set, and covering with foil after 10 minutes if the nuts are browning too quickly. Leave to cool in the tins for 10 minutes, then loosen with a round-bladed knife and transfer to a wire rack to cool.

6. For the decoration, put the chocolate in a heatproof bowl, set the bowl over a saucepan of gently simmering water and heat until melted. Dust the tops of the pies with a little sifted icing sugar. Spoon the chocolate into a paper piping bag, snip off the tip and pipe zigzag lines of melted chocolate over the pies, or drizzle the chocolate from a teaspoon. Leave the pies to set for 10 minutes, then arrange on a serving plate.

Pistachio and almond tarts

Makes: 12 mini muffin sized pies
Prep: 20 minutes
Cook: 15 minutes

A true French frangipane is made with just almonds, but a mixture of pretty green-tinged sliced pistachios and ground and flaked almonds makes for a luxurious mini pie.

225 g/8 oz Sweet Shortcrust
Pastry (see page 8) or
ready-made sweet shortcrust
pastry, chilled

a little plain flour, for dusting

50 g/1¾ oz butter, softened, plus
extra for greasing

50 g/1¾ oz caster sugar

1 egg yolk

50 g/1¾ oz ground almonds

a few drops of almond extract or
orange flower water

1½ tbsp flaked almonds

1 tbsp pistachio nuts, thinly sliced

a little icing sugar, sifted, to
decorate

1. Lightly grease a 12-section mini muffin tin. Preheat the oven to 180°C/350°F/Gas Mark 4.

2. Roll the pastry out thinly on a lightly floured surface. Using a fluted cookie cutter, stamp out 12 circles each 6 cm/2½ inches in diameter. Press these gently into the prepared tin, rerolling the trimmings as needed.

3. Meanwhile, put the butter and caster sugar in a mixing bowl and beat together until light and fluffy. Beat in the egg yolk, then the ground almonds. Flavour with a little almond essence or orange flower water.

4. Spoon the frangipane into the pastry cases.

5. Sprinkle the flaked almonds and sliced pistachios over the top and press them lightly into the filling.

6. Bake in the preheated oven for 15 minutes, or until the almonds are golden. Leave to cool in the tin for 10 minutes, then loosen with a round-bladed knife and transfer to a wire rack to cool. Serve warm or cold, dusted with sifted icing sugar.

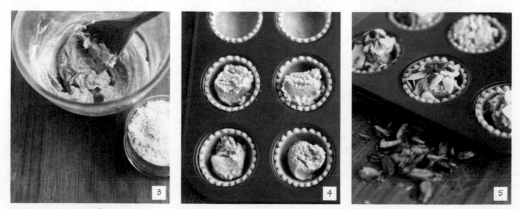

Coffee tarts

Makes: 12 muffin sized pies
Prep: 40 minutes
Cook: 27–33 minutes

Dark, rich and not overly sweet. Bite through a crisp buttery pie case to a coffee and dark chocolate custard topped with whipped cream flavoured with coffee cream liqueur. Delicious served with a cup of strong black coffee.

a little butter, for greasing

450 g/1 lb All Butter Pastry (see page 9) or ready-made sweet shortcrust pastry, chilled

a little plain flour, for dusting

225 ml/8 fl oz semi-skimmed milk

115 g/4 oz plain chocolate, roughly chopped

2 tsp instant coffee powder or granules

2 tbsp caster sugar

2 eggs

2 egg yolks

DECORATION

200 ml/7 fl oz double cream

2 tbsp icing sugar

2 tbsp coffee cream liqueur

1½ tsp instant coffee dissolved in 1 tsp boiling water

white chocolate curls, to decorate

a dusting of cocoa, sifted, to decorate

1. Lightly grease a 12-section muffin tin. Roll the pastry out thinly on a lightly floured surface. Using a plain cookie cutter, stamp out 12 circles each 10 cm/4 inches in diameter. Press these gently into the prepared tin, rerolling the trimmings as needed. Prick the base of each with a fork, then chill for 15 minutes. Preheat the oven to 190°C/375°F/Gas Mark 5.

2. Line the pastry cases with squares of crumpled baking paper and baking beans (see page 6). Bake in the preheated oven for 10 minutes. Remove the paper and beans and cook the cases for 2–3 minutes more, or until the base of the pastry is crisp. Turn the oven down to 160°C/325°F/Gas Mark 3. Meanwhile, bring the milk just to the boil in a small saucepan. Add the chocolate, coffee and caster sugar and leave to stand, off the heat, until the chocolate has melted.

3. Beat the eggs and yolks in a mixing bowl, then gradually whisk in the warm milk mixture until smooth. Pour the custard into the pastry cases.

4. Bake in the preheated oven for 15–20 minutes, or until just set. Leave to cool in the tin for 10 minutes, then loosen with a round-bladed knife and transfer to a wire rack. Whip the cream in a bowl until it forms soft swirls. Add the sugar, then whisk in the liqueur and coffee until thick. Spoon over the pies, then decorate with white chocolate curls and a dusting of cocoa.

Creamy Classics

Cherry cream pies

Makes: 12 muffin sized pies
Prep: 30 minutes
Cook: 25–30 minutes

These light cheese pies are perfect for a special summer picnic, although you may need to pack them with a little crumpled foil or kitchen roll to cushion any knocks. Serve with a spoonful of whipped cream flavoured with a little sugar and vanilla.

a little butter, for greasing

300 g/10½ oz mascarpone cheese

2 tsp plain flour, plus extra for dusting

85 g/3 oz caster sugar, plus extra for sprinkling

2 eggs

6 tbsp natural yogurt

1 tsp vanilla extract

450 g/1 lb All Butter Pastry (see page 9) or ready-made sweet shortcrust pastry, chilled

a little milk, to glaze

36 fresh or canned cherries, stoned and drained well

1. Lightly grease a 12-section muffin tin. Preheat the oven to 180°C/350°F/Gas Mark 4.

2. Spoon the mascarpone cheese into a mixing bowl and add the flour, sugar, eggs, yogurt and vanilla. Beat with a wooden spoon or electric hand-held whisk until just mixed.

3. Roll the pastry out thinly on a lightly floured surface. Using a plain cookie cutter, stamp out 12 circles each 10 cm/4 inches in diameter. Press these gently into the prepared tin, rerolling the trimmings as needed and reserving any remaining pastry. Brush the top edges of the pie cases with a little of the milk glaze and spoon in the filling. Add 3 cherries to each pie.

4. Roll the reserved pastry out thinly on a lightly floured surface. Cut strips about 1-cm/½-inch wide. Arrange 4 strips over each pie to make a lattice, pressing the edges together well to seal, then brush milk over the pastry and sprinkle with a little sugar.

5. Bake in the preheated oven for 25–30 minutes, or until the lattice is golden and the filling is just set. Leave to cool in the tin for 10 minutes, then loosen with a round-bladed knife and transfer to a wire rack to cool. Serve at room temperature.

Key lime pies

Makes: 24 mini muffin sized pies
Prep: 15 minutes
Cook: 6–8 minutes

4 tbsp golden syrup

70 g/2½ oz butter, plus extra for greasing

175 g/6 oz graham crackers or digestive biscuits, crushed

150 ml/5 fl oz double cream

grated rind of 2 limes

200 g/7 oz canned sweetened condensed milk

4 tbsp freshly squeezed limes (about 2 limes)

extra lime zest, to decorate

These super-speedy mini pies are filled with a luscious no-bake citrusy cream sweetened with condensed milk. They're great to make with kids.

1. Preheat the oven to 180°C/350°F/Gas Mark 4. Lightly grease 2 x 12-section mini muffin tins.

2. Put the syrup and butter in a small saucepan. Heat gently, uncovered, stirring, until the butter has just melted. Take the saucepan off the heat and stir in the biscuit crumbs. Divide the mixture between the sections of the prepared tins. Press it firmly over the base and sides of the tins with the back of a teaspoon.

3. Bake in the preheated oven for 6 minutes, or until slightly darker in colour. Reshape the centre if needed with the back of a spoon. Leave to cool and harden in the tins for 10–15 minutes.

4. Meanwhile, pour the cream into a bowl, add the lime rind and whisk until it is beginning to thicken. Gradually whisk in the condensed milk, then the lime juice, whisking for a few minutes more until it has thickened.

5. Pipe or spoon the lime cream into the cases. Chill for 30 minutes, or longer if you have time. Loosen the pies with a round-bladed knife and lift them carefully out of the tins. Decorate with lime zest curls.

Lemon and blueberry cheese pies

Makes: 12 muffin sized pies
Prep: 30 minutes
Cook: 23–30 minutes

Portions of cheesecake can be a struggle to wade through; not so with these morish individual pies. A tangy lemon cheesecake is held in a crisp chocolate crumb crust, then topped with slightly sharp soured cream and a blueberry compote. Depending on how many guests you have, or how big their appetites are, any leftover cheese pies can be frozen by wrapping each one in clingfilm and freezing the blueberry topping in a plastic container.

2 tbsp golden syrup

100 g/3½ oz butter, plus extra for greasing

300 g/10½ oz milk chocolate digestives or graham crackers, crushed

400 g/14 oz full-fat cream cheese

150 g/5½ oz caster sugar

150 ml/5 fl oz double cream

2 eggs

grated rind and juice of 1 lemon

400 g/14 oz blueberries

2 tsp cornflour

4 tbsp water

250 ml/9 fl oz crème fraîche

1. Preheat the oven to 180°C/350°F/Gas Mark 4. Lightly grease a 12-section muffin tin.

2. Put the syrup and butter in a small saucepan. Heat gently, uncovered, stirring, until the butter has just melted. Take the saucepan off the heat and stir in the biscuit crumbs. Divide the mixture between the sections of the prepared tin. Press it firmly over the base and sides of the tin using the back of a teaspoon.

3. Line the cases with baking paper and baking beans, then bake them in the preheated oven for 8–10 minutes, or until slightly darker in colour. Leave to cool and harden in the tin for 10–15 minutes. Remove the paper and beans. Turn the oven down to 150°F/300°F/Gas Mark 2.

4. Put the cream cheese into a mixing bowl. Add 115 g/4 oz of the sugar and beat together briefly with an electric handheld whisk. Gradually beat in the cream and then the eggs until smooth. Add the lemon rind, then stir in half the juice. Spoon the filling into the crumb cases.

5. Bake in the preheated oven for 15–20 minutes, or until the filling is just set with a slight wobble to the centre. Turn the oven off, open the door slightly and leave the pies to cool in the oven.

6. For the topping, put half the blueberries in a medium saucepan. Add the cornflour, remaining sugar and remaining lemon juice, then stir in the water. Cook over a low heat until the juice begins to run from the blueberries, then increase the heat and cook until the sauce has thickened. Add the remaining blueberries and cook for 2 minutes more. Take off the heat and leave to cool.

7. Loosen the pies with a round-bladed knife and transfer to a plate. Chill in the fridge for several hours. When ready to serve, top each with a spoonful of crème fraîche and a generous spoonful of the blueberries.

Christmas candied orange and meringue pies

Makes: 12 mini muffin sized pies
Prep: 35 minutes
Cook: 35 minutes

Cooking the clementine peel and flesh in a sugar syrup until soft and candied adds an almost marmalade-like sweet tangy flavour to these brown sugar meringue-topped pies.

a little butter, for greasing

225 g/8 oz Sweet Shortcrust Pastry (see page 8) or ready-made sweet shortcrust pastry, chilled

a little plain flour, for dusting

2 clementines or 1 small thin-skinned orange

85 g/3 oz caster sugar

150 ml/5 fl oz water

150 g/5½ oz ready-to-eat dried apricots, diced

2 egg whites

25 g/1 oz soft light brown sugar

orange rind curls, to decorate

1. Lightly grease a 12-section mini muffin tin. Preheat the oven to 180°C/350°F/Gas Mark 4.

2. Roll the pastry out thinly on a lightly floured surface. Using a fluted cookie cutter, stamp out 12 circles each 6 cm/2½ inches in diameter. Press these gently into the prepared tin, rerolling the trimmings as needed. Chill for 15 minutes.

3. Line the pastry cases with squares of crumpled baking paper and baking beans (see page 6). Bake in the preheated oven for 8 minutes. Remove the paper and beans and cook the cases for 2–3 minutes more, or until the base of the pastry is crisp and dry.

4. Meanwhile, peel the clementines and finely chop the rind. Separate the clementine segments, then roughly chop the flesh. Put the rind, two-thirds of the caster sugar and the water in a small saucepan, cover and simmer gently for 20 minutes. Add the flesh and the apricots and cook for 10 minutes more, or until soft and the water is driven off.

5. Spoon the orange filling into the pastry cases. Whisk the egg whites in a small clean mixing bowl until you have stiff, moist-looking peaks, then gradually whisk in the remaining caster sugar and the soft light brown sugar a teaspoon at a time for another 2 minutes, or until the meringue is very thick and glossy. Spoon or pipe the meringue onto the pies.

6. Bake in the preheated oven for 4–5 minutes, or until the meringue peaks are golden and just cooked through. Leave to cool in the tin for 10 minutes, then loosen with a round-bladed knife and transfer to a wire rack to cool. Serve warm, decorated with orange rind curls.

Maple cream pies with orange

Makes: 12 muffin sized pies
Prep: 45 minutes
Cook: 37–38 minutes

a little butter, for greasing

450 g/1 lb All Butter Pastry (see page 9) or ready-made sweet shortcrust pastry, chilled

a little plain flour, for dusting

225 ml/8 fl oz double cream

125 ml/4 fl oz maple syrup

2 eggs

2 egg yolks

grated rind of 1 orange

TO SERVE

3 oranges, peeled and segmented

3 tbsp maple syrup

Delicately flavoured creamy custard pies with a hint of maple and orange rind. Delicious served at room temperature, with extra orange segments and a drizzle of maple syrup.

1. Lightly grease a 12-section muffin tin. Roll the pastry out thinly on a lightly floured surface. Using a fluted cookie cutter, stamp out 12 circles, each 10 cm/4 inches in diameter. Press these gently into the prepared tin, rerolling the trimmings as needed. Prick the base of each with a fork, then chill in the fridge for 15 minutes. Preheat the oven to 190°C/375°F/Gas Mark 5.

2. Line the pastry cases with squares of crumpled baking paper and baking beans (see page 6). Bake in the preheated oven for 10 minutes. Remove the paper and beans and cook the pastry cases for 2–3 minutes more, or until the base of the pastry is crisp and dry. Turn the oven down to 160°C/325°F/Gas Mark 3.

3. Whisk the cream, syrup, eggs, egg yolks and most of the orange rind together in a jug. Pour this filling into the pie cases.

4. Bake in the preheated oven for 25 minutes, or until the custard is set. Leave to cool in the tins for 10 minutes, then loosen with a round-bladed knife and transfer to a serving plate.

5. Serve topped with extra orange segments, a sprinkling of the remaining grated orange rind and a drizzle of maple syrup.

Honey, walnut and ricotta pies

Makes: 24 mini muffin sized pies
Prep: 45 minutes
Cook: 25 minutes

Made here with a crisp, rich, all butter pastry, these would also taste great with cinnamon shortcrust. The perfect pie for those who don't have a sweet tooth. Undecorated pies will keep in the fridge for two to three days.

a little butter, for greasing

a little olive oil, for greasing

325 g/11½ oz All Butter Pastry (see page 9) or ready-made sweet shortcrust pastry, chilled

a little plain flour, for dusting

125 g/4½ oz walnut pieces

225 g/8 oz ricotta cheese

2 egg yolks

5 tbsp runny orange blossom honey

a large pinch of ground cinnamon

115 g/4 oz granulated sugar

1 tbsp water

200 g/7 oz Greek yogurt, to serve

1. Lightly grease 2 x 12-section mini muffin tins and oil a baking tray. Preheat the oven to 180°C/350°F/Gas Mark 4.

2. Roll the pastry out thinly on a lightly floured surface. Using a fluted cookie cutter, stamp out 24 circles each 6 cm/2½ inches in diameter. Press these gently into the prepared tins, rerolling the trimmings as needed.

3. Lightly toast half the walnut pieces in a dry non-stick frying pan. Leave them to cool, then roughly chop them.

4. Lightly whisk the ricotta, egg yolks, 4 tablespoons of the honey and the cinnamon together in a mixing bowl until just mixed. Stir in the toasted walnuts. Spoon the filling into the cases.

5. Bake in the preheated oven for 20 minutes, or until the filling is golden brown. Leave in the tin for 10 minutes to cool.

6. Meanwhile, for the praline put the sugar, remaining 1 tablespoon of honey and the water into the frying pan and heat gently without stirring until the sugar has dissolved. Tilt the pan to mix any remaining grains of sugar into the syrup. Add the remaining walnuts and cook over a medium heat, again without stirring, for about 5 minutes, or until the syrup turns a rich golden brown. Keep a watchful eye on the syrup as it will suddenly begin to change colour, darkening first around the edges. Tilt the pan to mix if needed, then quickly pour the praline onto the prepared baking tray and leave to cool and harden.

7. Loosen the pies with a round-bladed knife and transfer them to a plate. Just before serving, top them with spoonfuls of yogurt. Loosen the praline from the baking tray with a knife, then break or cut it into thin shards and press pieces of it into the yogurt.

Coconut cream pies

Makes: 12 muffin sized pies
Prep: 40 minutes
Cook: 8–10 minutes

An all-American favourite made with a coconut confectioners' custard and topped with vanilla cream. Ginger fans could try a little chopped crystallised stem ginger in the cream instead of the vanilla flavouring.

2 tbsp golden syrup

100 g/3½ oz butter, plus extra for greasing

300 g/10½ oz gingersnap or digestive biscuits, crushed

85 g/3 oz unsweetened desiccated coconut

125 ml/4 fl oz boiling water

55 g/2 oz caster sugar

20 g/¾ oz cornflour

20 g/¾ oz plain flour

2 egg yolks

300 ml/10 fl oz milk

grated rind of 1 lime

300 ml/10 fl oz double cream

1 tsp vanilla extract

2 tbsp icing sugar

toasted coconut curls or desiccated coconut

1. Preheat the oven to 180°C/350°F/Gas Mark 4. Lightly grease a 12-section muffin tin.

2. Put the syrup and butter in a small saucepan. Heat gently, uncovered, stirring, until the butter has just melted. Take the saucepan off the heat and stir in the biscuit crumbs. Divide the mixture between the sections of the prepared tin. Press it firmly over the base and sides of the tin with the back of a teaspoon.

3. Line the cases with baking paper and baking beans, then bake them in the preheated oven for 8–10 minutes, or until slightly darker in colour. Leave to cool and harden in the tin for 10–15 minutes. Remove the paper and beans.

4. Put the coconut into a mixing bowl and pour over the boiling water. Leave to stand for 10 minutes. Put the sugar, cornflour, plain flour and egg yolks in a separate mixing bowl and beat together.

5. Pour the milk into a small saucepan, bring just to the boil, then gradually whisk it into the egg yolk mixture until smooth. Return the milk mixture to the saucepan and cook over a medium heat, whisking, until thick. The sauce will suddenly thicken, and as it does you may find it easier to turn the heat right down to low so that you can whisk out any lumps quickly. Stir in the soaked coconut and the lime rind, cover the surface with wetted baking paper and leave to cool.

6. Loosen the pie cases with a round-bladed knife and carefully lift out of the tin. Spoon in the coconut filling.

7. Whip the cream until it just forms soft swirls, then fold in the vanilla extract and sugar. Spoon this over the tops of the pies, then decorate with coconut curls or desiccated coconut.

Super Savouries

Steak and ale pies

Makes: 12 muffin sized pies
Prep: 30 minutes
Cook: 30–35 minutes

1 tbsp olive oil

15 g/½ oz salted butter, plus extra
for greasing

500 g/1 lb 2 oz sirloin or rump
steak, fat discarded and meat cut
into 2.5-cm/1-inch cubes

2 shallots, finely chopped

150 g/5½ oz button mushrooms,
sliced

1 bay leaf

1 tbsp plain flour, plus extra for
dusting

225 ml/8 fl oz brown ale

125 ml/4 fl oz beef stock

1 tbsp tomato purée

1 quantity Mustard Shortcrust
Pastry (see pages 8–9), or 650 g/
1 lb 7 oz ready-made
shortcrust pastry, chilled

1 egg yolk mixed with 1 tbsp
water, to glaze

salt flakes and pepper

Adding a little dried English mustard to the pastry gives these pies a wonderful colour and flavour and complements their full-bodied filling. If you are short of time, ready-made shortcrust pastry will work just as well.

1. Preheat the oven to 180°C/350°F/Gas Mark 4. Lightly grease a 12-section muffin tin.

2. To make the filling, heat the oil and butter in a frying pan over a medium heat. Add the steak, finely chopped shallots, mushrooms and bay and fry, stirring, until the steak is evenly browned and the shallots are golden brown.

3. Sprinkle the flour over the top, mix together, then add the brown ale, stock, tomato purée and a little salt and pepper. Simmer for 5 minutes, stirring from time to time, until the sauce has thickened. Leave to cool, then remove the bay.

4. Roll two-thirds of the pastry out thinly on a lightly floured surface. Using a plain cookie cutter, stamp out 12 circles each 10 cm/4 inches in diameter. Press these gently into the prepared muffin tin, rerolling the trimmings as needed.

5. Brush the top edges of the pie cases with a little of the egg glaze, then spoon in the filling.

6. Roll out the reserved pastry and any trimmings on a lightly floured surface. Using a plain cookie cutter, stamp out 12 circles each 7 cm/3 inches in diameter for the pie lids. Arrange these on top of the pies, pressing the edges together well with the tines of a fork to seal. Brush egg glaze over the pastry. Sprinkle with a little salt and pepper.

7. Bake in the preheated oven for 25 minutes, or until the pastry is golden. Leave to cool in the tins for 5 minutes, then loosen with a round-bladed knife and transfer to a wire rack.

Lamb and rosemary pasties

Makes: 12 mini pasties
Prep: 30 minutes
Cook: 37–38 minutes

2 tbsp olive oil

450 g/1 lb lean leg of lamb or
lamb fillet, cut into
1 cm/½ inch cubes

200 g/7 oz potato, diced

6 spring onions, finely chopped

2 garlic cloves, finely chopped

150 g/5 oz cherry tomatoes,
halved

1 quantity Herb Shortcrust Pastry
(see pages 8–9), or
650 g/1 lb 7 oz ready-made
shortcrust pastry, chilled

a little plain flour, for dusting

1 egg yolk mixed with 1 tbsp
water, to glaze

salt flakes and pepper

rosemary sprigs, to garnish

These rustic little hand-shaped pies are great for an informal weekend lunch while out working out in the garden.

1. Preheat the oven to 180°C/350°F/Gas Mark 4. Line a large baking sheet with non-stick baking paper.

2. Heat the oil in a frying pan over a medium heat. Add the lamb and potato and fry, stirring, for 10 minutes, or until the lamb is browned and the potato just tender. Add the spring onions, garlic, tomatoes and plenty of salt and pepper and cook for 2–3 minutes more, or until the tomatoes are just beginning to soften, then leave to cool.

3. Roll the pastry out thinly on a lightly floured surface. Using a plain cookie cutter, stamp out 12 circles each 12.5 cm/5 inches in diameter, rerolling the trimmings as needed.

4. Spoon the filling into the centre of each circle, then brush the edges of the pastry with a little of the egg glaze.

5. Fold the pastry over the filling to make half-moon-shaped pasties, pressing the edges together well to seal. Roll the edge, then mark with a knife. Transfer the pasties to the prepared baking sheet, brush them with egg and sprinkle with a some salt flakes and a few rosemary sprigs.

6. Bake in the preheated oven for 25 minutes, or until the pies are golden. Leave to cool on the baking sheet for 5 minutes, then serve hot or cold, sprinkled with flaked salt.

Chicken pot pies

Makes: 12 muffin sized pies
Prep: 30 minutes
Cook: 42 minutes

25 g/1 oz salted butter, plus extra
for greasing

1 tbsp olive oil

500 g/1 lb 2 oz boneless, skinless
chicken breasts, cut into
1 cm/½ inch cubes

1 leek, about 175 g/6 oz, thinly
sliced, white and green slices
kept separate

2 tbsp plain flour, plus extra for
dusting

450 ml/16 fl oz chicken stock

4 tbsp Noilly Pratt or dry white
wine

2 tbsp roughly chopped fresh
tarragon

2 tbsp roughly chopped fresh
parsley

1 tbsp chopped capers

1 quantity Savoury Shortcrust
Pastry (see page 8) or 650 g/1 lb
7 oz ready-made plain shortcrust
pastry, chilled

1 egg yolk mixed with 1 tbsp
water, to glaze

salt and pepper

blanched asparagus, to serve

These dainty pies are ideal for a girlie lunch. If you are feeling extra hungry you may have room for two. If not the kids will be happy to devour any leftovers when they come back from school ravenous.

1. Preheat the oven to 180°C/350°F/Gas Mark 4. Lightly grease a 12-section muffin tin.

2. Heat the butter and oil in a frying pan over a medium heat. Add the chicken and white sliced leeks and fry, stirring, for 10 minutes, or until the chicken is golden brown and the leeks are softened.

3. Sprinkle the flour over the top, mix together, then add the stock, Noilly Pratt and a little salt and pepper. Simmer for 5 minutes, stirring from time to time, until the sauce has thickened and the chicken is cooked through. Add the green leek slices and cook for 2 minutes, or until the leeks are just soft. Sprinkle over the tarragon, parsley and capers and leave to cool.

4. Roll two-thirds of the pastry out thinly on a lightly floured surface. Using a plain cookie cutter, stamp out 12 circles each 10 cm/4 inches in diameter. Press these gently into the prepared muffin tin, rerolling the trimmings as needed.

5. Brush the top edges of the pie cases with a little of the egg glaze, then spoon in the filling.

6. Roll out the reserved pastry and any trimmings on a lightly floured surface. Using a plain cookie cutter, stamp out 12 circles each 7 cm/3 inches in diameter. Arrange these on top of the pies, pressing the edges together well to seal. Decorate the pastry edge by pressing it between the finger and thumb of your left hand and then pressing the edge with your right index finger or a small knife to make a scalloped pattern. Brush the pastry with egg glaze; add leaves cut out from rolled pastry trimmings using a sharp knife, then brush these with egg too.

7. Bake in the preheated oven for 25 minutes, or until golden brown. Leave to cool in the tin for 5 minutes, then loosen with a round-bladed knife and transfer to serving plates. Serve hot or cold with asparagus.

Turkey pies with cranberry and red onion relish

Makes: 12 muffin sized pies
Prep: 20 minutes
Cook: 33-34 minutes

300 g/10½ oz Savoury Shortcrust Pastry (see page 8) or ready-made shortcrust pastry, chilled

a little plain flour, for dusting

1 egg yolk mixed with 1 tbsp water, to glaze

300 g/10½ oz minced turkey

4 spring onions, finely chopped

2 garlic cloves, finely chopped

4 stems fresh thyme, leaves torn from stems

1 tsp ground allspice

2 egg yolks

salt and cayenne pepper

TO GARNISH

1 tbsp olive oil

1 red onion, thinly sliced

85 g/3 oz frozen cranberries

3 tbsp cranberry sauce

4 tbsp ruby Port or red wine

These mini pies make great snacks that the family can help themselves to from the fridge, as and when they get peckish.

1. Preheat the oven to 180°C/350°F/Gas Mark 4. Line a 12-section muffin tin with squares of non-stick baking paper.

2. Roll the pastry out thinly on a lightly floured surface. Using a plain cookie cutter, stamp out 12 circles each 12.5 cm/5 inches in diameter. Press these gently into the prepared muffin tin, so the pastry stands just above the top of the tin in soft pleats, rerolling the trimmings as needed.

3. Brush the top edges of the pie cases with a little of the egg glaze.

4. Put the turkey, onions, garlic and thyme leaves into a mixing bowl. Sprinkle over the allspice and a little salt and cayenne pepper, then stir in the egg yolks until well mixed. Spoon the filling into the pie cases and press the tops flat with the back of a teaspoon.

5. Bake in the preheated oven for 30 minutes, or until the pastry is golden and the filling is cooked through. Leave to cool in the tins for 5 minutes, then loosen with a round-bladed knife and transfer to a wire rack.

6. Meanwhile, for the garnish, heat the oil in a frying pan, add the red onion and cook until just beginning to soften. Add the remaining ingredients and cook for 3-4 minutes, or until the cranberries are soft. Spoon over the top of the baked pies and serve.

Salmon pies with dill gremolata

Makes: 12 muffin sized pies
Prep: 30 minutes
Cook: 15 minutes

Bite through a thin buttery filo case to a rich creamy sauce extravagantly filled with moist chunks of fresh salmon. Seafood fans may like to add prawns or flavour the sauce with dark crab meat and add the white crab meat towards the end of cooking.

40 g/1½ oz salted butter, plus extra for greasing

3 x 48-cm x 25-cm/19-inch x 10-inch sheets frozen filo pastry, defrosted

FILLING

2 salmon steaks, about 350 g/12 oz in total

300 ml/10 fl oz semi-skimmed milk

25 g/1 oz salted butter

6 spring onions, thinly sliced

25 g/1 oz plain flour

2 tbsp crème fraîche

2 tbsp Noilly Pratt, dry white wine or dry sherry

2 tbsp roughly chopped fresh dill

grated rind of 1 lemon

salt and pepper

1. Preheat the oven to 180°C/350°F/Gas Mark 4. Lightly grease a 12-section muffin tin. Put the butter into a small saucepan and heat until it has just melted.

2. Unfold 1 sheet of pastry, brush it with a little melted butter, then cut it into 8 pieces, each 12-cm/4½-inches square. Press 1 piece into a section of the prepared tin, then layer a second piece on top at right angles to the first. Continue in the remaining sections, with the remaining filo, until you have 12 x 2-layer cases. Roll the top edges down to make a pie crust.

3. Bake in the preheated oven for 5 minutes, or until golden and crisp, then lift the cases out of the tin and put them onto a plate.

4. Meanwhile, put the salmon in a medium saucepan, pour over the milk and season with a little salt and pepper. Cover and simmer gently for 10 minutes, or until the fish is just cooked. Lift the fish out of the milk, pour the milk into a jug and reserve, then wash and dry the pan.

5. Heat the butter in the pan until melted, then add the spring onions and fry for 2 minutes, or until just softened. Stir in the flour, cook 1 minute more, then gradually mix in the reserved milk plus the crème fraîche and Noilly Pratt and bring to the boil, stirring until thickened and smooth.

6. Flake the fish into chunky pieces, discarding any skin and bones. Add the flakes of fish to the sauce and reheat if needed. Spoon the hot filling into the pastry cases, then mix the dill and lemon rind together and sprinkle over the top.

Egg and sunblush tomato pies

Makes: 12 muffin sized pies
Prep: 30 minutes
Cook: 20 minutes

a little butter, for greasing

450 g/1 lb Savoury
Shortcrust Pastry (see page 8)
or ready-made shortcrust pastry,
chilled

a little plain flour, for dusting

4 eggs

150 ml/5 fl oz milk

6 spring onions, finely chopped

2 tbsp roughly chopped fresh
basil

175 g/6 oz brie, diced

100 g/3½ oz sunblush tomatoes,
finely sliced

salt and pepper

These deep-dish pies have a quiche-style filling flavoured with sunblush tomatoes and brie. They're perfect for family picnics or packing into work or school lunchboxes.

1. Preheat the oven to 180°C/350°F/Gas Mark 4. Lightly grease a 12-section muffin tin.

2. Roll the pastry out thinly on a lightly floured surface. Using a plain cookie cutter, stamp out 12 circles each 10 cm/4 inches in diameter. Press these gently into the prepared muffin tin, rerolling the pastry trimmings as needed.

3. Put the eggs, milk and a little salt and pepper together in a large jug and beat lightly with a fork. Mix in the onions and basil. Pour the filling into the pie cases, then sprinkle the brie and tomatoes on top.

4. Bake in the preheated oven for 20 minutes, or until the pastry is golden and the filling is set. Leave to cool in the tin for 10 minutes, then loosen with a round-bladed knife and transfer to a wire rack.

Mini Greek spinach and pine nut pies

Makes: 12 muffin sized pies
Prep: 20 minutes
Cook: 20-25 minutes

55 g/2 oz salted butter, plus extra
for greasing

4 x 48-cm x 25-cm/19-inch
x 10-inch sheets of frozen filo
pastry, defrosted

FILLING

250 g/9 oz baby spinach leaves,
rinsed with cold water and
drained

1 tbsp olive oil

1 small onion, finely chopped

2 garlic cloves, finely chopped

100 g/3½ oz feta cheese, drained
and grated

200 g/7 oz medium-fat soft
cheese

2 eggs

a little grated nutmeg

salt and pepper

3 tbsp pine nuts, to garnish

*These Greek-inspired pies are great to offer to
visiting veggie friends, but be sure to check the cheese
carries the vegetarian symbol.*

1. Preheat the oven to 180°C/350°F/Gas Mark 4. Lightly grease
a 12-section muffin tin.

2. To make the filling, preheat a frying pan over a medium heat. Add the
spinach and stir fry for 2-3 minutes, or until just wilted. Scoop it out of the
pan, add it to a large sieve and press out any remaining liquid. Heat the oil
in the empty pan, add the onion and garlic and fry over a medium heat
until softened.

3. Put the feta and soft cheese in a mixing bowl. Stir, then beat in the eggs
one at a time and season with nutmeg, salt and pepper. Finely chop the
spinach and stir this and the onion and garlic in too.

4. For the pastry cases, put the butter into a small saucepan and heat until
it has just melted.

5. Unfold 1 sheet of pastry, brush it with a little melted butter, then cut it
into 8 pieces, each 12 cm/4½ inches square. Press 1 piece into a section of
the prepared tin, then layer a second piece on top at right angles to the first.
Continue like this in the remaining sections, with 2 more sheets of filo, until
you have 12 x 2-layer cases.

6. Divide the spinach filling between the pies. Fold the edges of the
pastry over the filling. Tear strips from the remaining pastry sheet, crumple
this over the top of the pies, brush with the remaining butter and sprinkle
on the pine nuts.

7. Bake in the preheated oven for 20-25 minutes, or until the pastry is
golden and pies have risen slightly. Check on the pies after 15 minutes and
cover with foil if the nuts seem to be browning too quickly. Leave to cool in
the tin for 10 minutes, then loosen with a round-bladed knife and transfer to
a serving plate. Serve warm or cold.

Index